MIND-BLOWING ☑LISTS ABOUT TECHNOLOGY

Heather E. Schwartz

CAPSTONE PRESS
a capstone imprint

Published by Capstone Press, an imprint of Capstone
1710 Roe Crest Drive,
North Mankato, Minnesota 56003
capstonepub.com

Copyright © 2026 by Capstone. All rights reserved. No part of this publication may be reproduced in whole or in part, or stored in a retrieval system, or transmitted in any form or by any means, electronic, mechanical, photocopying, recording, or otherwise, without written permission of the publisher.

Library of Congress Cataloging-in-Publication Data is available on the Library of Congress website.

ISBN: 9798875228254 (hardcover)
ISBN: 9798875231872 (paperback)
ISBN: 9798875231889 (ebook PDF)

Summary: From the invention of the wheel to the latest smartphone features, technology has been an important part of human history for thousands of years. Easy-to-read lists featuring fascinating and surprising tech facts are sorted into clear chapters that encourage both reluctant readers and information-seekers alike. Full-color images, fun designs, and amazing facts will get kids' minds moving.

Editorial Credits
Editor: Marissa Bolte; Designer: Kay Fraser;
Media Researcher: Svetlana Zhurkin;
Production Specialist: Katy LaVigne

Image Credits
Capstone: Kay Fraser (design elements), cover and throughout; Getty Images: akwitps, 18, Bertl123, cover (bottom left), 8, David C Tomlinson, 23, dima_zel, cover (ISS and Mars rover), 26, Dorling Kindersley, 17, Prykhodov, cover (smartphone), 15; Newscom: AFLO/Richard Atrero de Guzman, 30, Imagine China, 31; Shutterstock: 3DMI, 27, Agia, 22, Alina Cardiae Photography, cover (traffic lights), anek.soowannaphoom, 9, DFabri, 13, encierro, 6, FooTToo, 12, Fusionstudio, 14, Georgios Tsichlis, 7 (top), Hasan Shaheed, 10, Hethers, 28, I Wei Huang, 5, Jouni Niskakoski, 25, Maxshot, 16, Melica, 21, MikeDotta, 29, Peter Hermes Furian, 24, pmvfoto, 4, Proxima Studio, 20, solarseven, 7 (bottom), TarasBeletskiy, cover (record player), 19, Viliam.M, 11

Any additional websites and resources referenced in this book are not maintained, authorized, or sponsored by Capstone. All product and company names are trademarks™ or registered® trademarks of their respective holders.

Printed and bound in the USA. 6307

TABLE OF CONTENTS

CHAPTER 1
EARLIEST INVENTIONS 4

CHAPTER 2
ELECTRIC INVENTIONS 14

CHAPTER 3
TRAVEL TECH 22

CHAPTER 4
ROBOTIC WONDERS 28

CHAPTER 1
EARLIEST INVENTIONS

Today's tech is pretty impressive. But some of the earliest inventions were incredible too. The first tools were made of stone and used for cooking. That was more than 3 million years ago! People have been thinking up new ways to make life easier ever since.

USE TOOLS MADE FROM...

- stone
- iron
- wood
- copper

HUNT WITH...

- bow and arrow
- spear
- fishhook
- blowpipe

COOK DINNER WITH...

- spits—long rods used to hold and turn food
- clay ovens—dome-shaped ovens made of clay
- smoke—using fire and smoke to flavor, preserve, or brown food
- open fires—outdoor fires made using firewood or charcoal
- metal cauldrons—large, round metal cooking pots

FIND THE WAY WITH...

- maps carved in stone
- compasses, which use magnets to tell directions
- backstaffs, which use shadows to measure the height of the sun
- globes that model the known world
- sextants, which use angles to measure distances between two objects, like the sun and the horizon

KEEP TRACK OF TIME WITH...

- sundials
- candles
- water clocks
- calendars

ANCIENT EGYPTIAN INVENTIONS

- breath mints
- toothpaste
- door locks
- makeup
- wigs

ANCIENT INDIAN INVENTIONS

- buttons
- shampoo
- ink
- flushing toilets
- chess

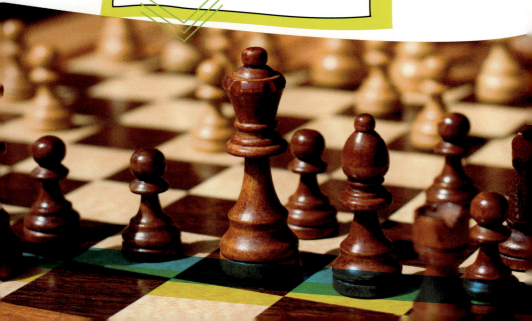

ANCIENT GREEK INVENTIONS

- stone arch bridges
- catapults
- cranes
- syringes

ANCIENT CHINESE INVENTIONS

- gunpowder
- fireworks
- compasses
- printing

ROUND AND ROUND

Wheels are so useful!

- 3500 BCE—wheels first helped people get around
- 2400 BCE—potter's wheel gets popular, making it easier to make containers to hold food, water, and other valuable items
- 450 BCE—water mills made grinding grain to flour easier

TIME-TESTED WATER TECH

- 8,000 years ago—dowsing to find underground water
- 2,520 years ago—water filters
- 2,400 years ago—flush toilets
- 2,336 years ago—aqueducts used to bring water into cities

WIND ENERGY TECH

- wind catcher—catches air for cooling
- wind pump—a wind-powered water pump
- windmill and wind turbine—wind moves the blades, which collect energy to use later
- sail—a large piece of cloth that catches wind to move a boat

PRE-TABLET TECH

- hornbook—a wooden paddle with the alphabet and phrases glued onto it
- slate—a small blackboard made of slate stone
- slate pencil—a writing tool that could write on slate
- chalkboard—a dark surface that can be written on with chalk
- chalk—a soft white rock for writing
- quill pen—a writing tool made from a bird's feather

EARLY MUSICAL INSTRUMENTS

- sackbut—similar to today's trombone
- serpent—a snakelike bass wind instrument
- dulcian—an early version of the bassoon
- rackett—a reed instrument so small it's also called a pocket bassoon
- crumhorn—a wind instrument that sounds like a bagpipe
- theorbo—a long-necked bass lute, with strings like a guitar
- shawm—an early oboe
- glass armonica—a set of large-to-small tuned glass bowls
- drum—a hollow instrument played by hand or with sticks

WRITE IT DOWN

- 3200 BCE—first record of written language
- 3100 BCE—clay tablets
- 2900 BCE—papyrus, a material made from plants
- 2568 BCE—scrolls, made from papyrus, silk, or animal skins
- 2500 BCE—black ink, made from soot and water
- 1450 CE—movable type printing press

MILITARY TECH

- gunpowder
- cannon
- iron-casting
- armor

MATHEMATICAL DISCOVERIES

Some discoveries have changed the way we do math today. Other discoveries are still ongoing!

- the concept of zero
- the abacus (the calculator's earliest ancestor)
- the Fibonacci Sequence, also known as the "Golden Ratio," which is used to see and create patterns: 0, 1, 1, 2, 3, 5, 8, 13, 21, 34, 55, 89, 144, 233, 377, 610, 987, 1597, 2584, 4181, 6765, 10946, 17711 . . .
- Pi, which is used to measure circles: 3.14159265358979323846264 3383279502884197 . . .

EARLY TOILETS

- bushes
- public latrines
- outhouses
- chamber pots

EARLY TOILET PAPER TECH

- seashells
- a sponge on a stick
- moss
- leaves
- pieces of pottery
- a spatula
- animal furs
- hay or corncobs

TOP TEN EARLY TOOTHPASTES

A little bit of these powdered ingredients went a long way to clean teeth.

- oxen hooves
- myrrh (a gum from trees)
- eggshells
- pumice (a volcanic rock)
- snail shells
- oyster shells
- orris root (the root of an iris)
- charcoal
- Peruvian bark
- gypsum (a mineral)

TECH THAT WAS ONCE DENTIST APPROVED

- chew stick (a stick that was frayed on one end for brushing and sharp on the other end for picking)
- slivers of wood
- slivers of bone
- porcupine quills
- crow quills

CHAPTER 2
ELECTRIC INVENTIONS

The first observation of electricity dates back to 600 BCE. People couldn't use it in their homes until 1882, though. Can you imagine your life without it?

HOT TECH

- oven
- stovetop
- microwave
- furnace
- electric blanket

COOL TECH
- fan
- air conditioner
- refrigerator
- refrigerated van
- ice cream truck

TOP 5 ELECTRIC INVENTIONS
- lightbulb
- battery
- hearing aid
- smartphone
- internet

NOTEWORTHY INVENTORS
- Allesandro Volta—electric battery (1808)
- Alexander Miles—automatic elevator doors (1887)
- Mary Anderson—windshield wipers (1903)
- Garrett Morgan—three-position traffic signal (1923)

FUN TECH THROUGH TIME

- 1816—camera
- 1874—electric keyboard
- 1958—video games
- 1980—laptop
- 1993—streaming
- 1994—smart TV

TIMELINE OF COMMUNICATION INVENTIONS

- 1838—telegraph
- 1860—Pony Express
- 1876—telephone
- 1895—radio
- 1927—television
- 1971—email
- 1973—wireless phone
- 1992—texting

PHONES THROUGH THE AGES

- 1876—landline
- 1879—top box
- 1889—pay
- 1891—rotary
- 1927—video
- 1946—car
- 1956—cordless
- 1959—princess
- 1963—touch-tone
- 1989—satellite
- 1992—smartphone

OLD-TIMEY TELEPHONES

- telegraph—Send a message using dots and dashes!

- fax—The original email used phone lines to send a copy of a document.

- pager or beeper—Check your messages! A pager told people when someone had called from a specific phone number.

- party line—How would you like to share a phone number with your neighbors?

- CB radio—Can you hear me? Over!

- ham radio—Meet friends on a specific radio frequency and chat all night.

VINTAGE MUSIC TECH

- transistor radio
- 8-track tape
- cassette tape
- boombox
- CD (compact disc)
- portable CD player
- record player

RETRO COMPUTER TECH

- dial-up modem
- floppy disk
- dot-matrix printer

OLD-SCHOOL MOVIE PLAYERS

- 8mm reel-to-reel tape
- VHS (Video Home System) cassette tape
- Betamax cassette tape
- portable TV
- DVD (digital versatile disc)
- LaserDisc

THAT'S SMART!

Smart inventions use technology similar to artificial intelligence (AI) to help people with tasks. They are connected to the internet. People can control them even when they're not at home!

SMART TECH AROUND THE HOUSE

- speaker
- garage door opener
- doorbell
- lightbulb
- door lock
- thermostat
- voice-activated light
- TV

SMART KITCHEN TECH

These smart devices can be set to turn on and off automatically, remind users to shop for supplies, and even cook a whole turkey.

- coffee maker
- oven
- air fryer
- ice maker
- refrigerator

SMART BATHROOM TECH

- warming drawer—keeps towels toasty
- shower—sets the temperature just right
- mirror—tells the time, date, weather, and more
- voice-activated fan—turns on and off without a switch
- touchless toilet—can be flushed with the wave of a hand
- faucet—activates without a touch and even tracks water usage
- bathmat—tracks posture, balance, and body weight
- waterproof TV—can go right in the shower

CHAPTER 3

Thanks to planes, boats, and other transportation technology, we can go *almost* anywhere.

FIVE SUPER-FAST CARS

- Koenigsegg Agera RS—278 miles (447.4 kilometers) per hour
- Bugatti Chiron Super Sport—273 miles (439.4 km) per hour
- 9ff GT9—272 miles (437.7 km) per hour
- Czinger 21C—253 miles (407 km) per hour
- Hennessey Venom GT—270.5 miles (435.3 km) per hour

WORLD'S LONGEST TRAINS

- Mt. Goldsworthy—4.5 miles (7.2 km) long
- Vale—2 miles (3.2 km) long
- Shenhua No. 3—1.6 miles (2.6 km) long
- Train du Desert—1.5 miles (2.4 km) long
- The Ghan—0.7 miles (1.1 km) long
- Indian Pacific—0.5 miles (0.8 km) long
- Shinkansen N700 "Bullet Train"—0.25 miles (0.4 km) long

OLDEST TRAINS STILL IN SERVICE

- 1862—Flying Scotsman
- 1883—Orient Express
- 1887—The Overland
- 1887—Sud Express
- 1889—Punjab Mail
- 1891—Crescent
- 1894—Sunset Limited
- 1904—Ocean
- 1904—Cornish Riviera Express
- 1910—Bernina Express

ARE WE THERE YET?

Without roads, getting places would be much, much slower. Some routes stretch a mile or two. Others go on forever! How far can you go on a single road trip?

- London, England, to Cape Town, South Africa—10,000 miles (16,093.4 km)
- Sagres, Portugal, to Talon, Russia—9,414 miles (15,150 km)
- North Quoddy, Maine, to Sumas, Washington—3,490 miles (5,616 km)

TOP 5 BIGGEST CRUISE SHIPS

- 5. *Wonder of the Seas*—1,187 feet (362 meters)
- 4. *Allure of the Seas*—1,187 feet (362 m)
- 3. *Harmony of the Seas*—1,188 feet (362 m)
- 2. *Utopia of the Seas*—1,188 feet (362 m)
- 1. *Icon of the Seas*—1,197 feet (365 m)

MOST REMOTE ISLANDS

Find each of these places on a map. What tech would you need to travel there?

- Kerguelen Islands—sub-Antarctic region
- Spitsbergen—Arctic Ocean near Norway
- Pitcairn Island—Southern Pacific Ocean
- Novaya Zemlya—Arctic Ocean near Russia
- Tristan da Cunha—South Atlantic Ocean
- Easter Island—southeastern Pacific Ocean
- South Georgia—South Atlantic Ocean
- Diego Garcia—British Indian Ocean Territory

TAKE A TRIP TO SPACE

So far, space tourism is taking regular people to the edge of outer space. Some trips are quick, lasting only a minute or two. Others take travelers to eat, sleep, and stay in space!

- $55 million—SpaceX (one week in space with a private crew)
- $28 million—Blue Origin (10 minutes at the edge of space)
- $5 million—Voyager Station (three days in space)
- $495,000—SpaceVIP (dine at the edge of space)
- $450,000—Virgin Galactic (two to three hours at the edge of space)
- $210,000—Deep Blue Aerospace (12 minutes at the edge of space)
- $125,000—Space Perspective (six hours at the edge of space)
- $35,000—NASA (one night on the International Space Station)

RED PLANET ROVERS

NASA's Mars rovers have paved the way for human visits in the future.

- Sojourner
- Perseverance
- Spirit
- Opportunity
- Curiosity

CHAPTER 4
ROBOTIC WONDERS

Once, robots were just an idea on sci-fi TV shows. Today, they're commonplace technology!

SCI-FI ROBOTS IN BOOKS

- Robot from *Nufonia Must Fall*
- Marvin from *The Hitchhiker's Guide to the Galaxy*
- Tik-Tok from *The Wizard of Oz*
- HAL 9000 from *2001: A Space Odyssey*

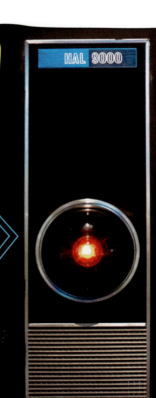

REAL-LIFE HELPFUL ROBOTS

- Edinburgh Modular Arm System—the world's first bionic arm
- exoskeletons—wearable structures that support movement
- ElliQ—a device that keeps seniors connected with family and friends
- Spot—a robot dog that helps firefighters
- Roomba—a room-cleaning robot
- robo-fish—robots that remove microplastics from oceans
- brain-reading robots—computer robots that help injured people move by reading their brainwaves

THE ROBOT ZOO

- BellaBot—a cat that takes your dinner order
- PARO—a seal that helps people in therapy
- Qoobo—a cushion with a wagging tail that reacts to touch and sound
- Yume Neko Smile—a toy cat
- Robear—a bear that helps elderly patients at home
- Kiki—a dog to be your new (robotic) best friend

SMALLEST AND BIGGEST

- 0.0098 inches (0.02 centimeters)—smallest untethered robot
- 0.02 inches (0.5 millimeters)—peekytoe crab robot
- 5.5 inches (14 cm)—smallest humanoid robot
- 28 feet (8.5 meters)—MONONOFU, the largest mobile humanoid robot

BOT COMPETITIONS

- RoboCup
- Robot Combat League
- Robot-Sumo

HUMANLIKE ROBOTS

These robots can hold conversations and answer questions or offer help. They can move their heads, blink, and use facial expressions to let listeners know how they're feeling.

- Sophia
- Ameca
- Grace
- Jia Jia
- Nadine

SPORTY ROBOTS

- CUE—a basketball robot that can dribble and shoot hoops
- Jennifer—a robot that can downhill and cross-country ski, and play hockey
- Atlas—a robot that can do a whole gymnastics routine
- FORPHEUS—a robot that uses motion sensors to play table tennis

MORE INFO FANATIC BOOKS!

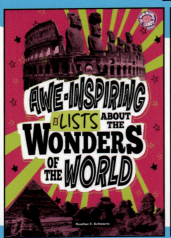
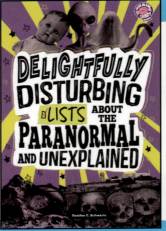
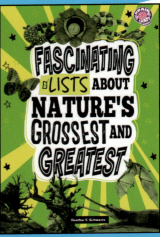

ABOUT THE AUTHOR

Heather E. Schwartz is an author, singer, and performance artist based in upstate New York. She loves writing because she loves learning new things and brainstorming creative ideas. A few sights she would like to see from this series include Cat Island, mammatus clouds, and Prada Marfa. She'd rather not experience spider rain! She lives with her husband and two kids, and their cats, Stampy and Squid.